Positive Afrikan Images for Children

The Council of Independent Black Institutions (CIBI) Social Studies Curriculum

Positive Afrikan Images for Children

Social Studies Curriculum

The Council of Independent
Black Institutions
(CIBI)

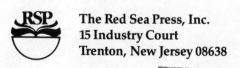

The Red Sea Press, Inc.
15 Industry Court
Trenton, New Jersey 08638

THE RED SEA PRESS, INC.
15 INDUSTRY COURT
TRENTON, NEW JERSEY 08638

Cover Art by Afia Akoto

Library of Congress Catalog Card Number: 90-60173

ISBN: 0-932415-48-2 Paper

Acknowledgements

Curricula, by definition, are dynamic, with subject content and instructional methodology constantly changing and adapting to the social and political circumstances in our communities. Social studies is probably the most variable of the formal academic areas, as it is directly and immediately affected by the dynamics of contemporary society. The very name "social studies" implies collective and coordinated actions to accomplish a mission.

The completion of the CIBI Social Studies Curriculum Guide, has required just such an effort. This work is the product of the effort to construct a core social studies curriculum for institutional members of the Council of Independent Black Institutions. The task of research, writing, and editing over many long hours was undertaken in the true spirit of Ujima (Collective Work & Responsibility). Those institutions whose energies made this work possible include NationHouse Positive Action Center (Curriculum Development Office for CIBI), Afrikan Peoples' Action School, New Concept Development Center, Omowale Ujamaa, and Shule Ya Watoto. The completion of the curriculum guide owes much to the splendid efforts of artist Afia Akoto, and to the composition and typesetting of sister Esi Rehema. The foresight, persistence and leadership of Hannibal Afrik, Mwalimu Shujaa and Kofi Lomotey have been equally crucial in the completion of this work.

It can be safely stated that all involved pray that their collective efforts bear the fruit of enlightenment and commitment in the minds and hearts of our children.

Agyei Akoto,
Project Coordinator,
NationHouse Positive Action Center

THE COUNCIL OF INDEPENDENT BLACK INSTITUTIONS (CIBI) SOCIAL STUDIES CURRICULUM

Social studies, more than any other area of study, shapes the cultural and ideological perspectives of the developing child. Social studies is a comprehensive area of study which includes subject content from history, geography, civics, political science, economics, government, and anthropology. Given the breadth of the social studies curriculum and dynamic nature of human societies, much of the content will change as society changes. This curriculum guide has been designed to facilitate the cultural development of the Afrikan American child. It has been designed to foster the firm self concept and clear sense of direction and purpose that attends a culturally appropriate curriculum design and a self reflective learning environment. Though the curriculum is Afrikan centered, its content and design do not prejudge or understate the significance of other cultures. It does, however, firmly place the cultural dynamic of Afrikan people in its proper place among the world's cultures.

The social studies curriculum guide presented here consists of three components. The first component consists of working definitions and important concepts concerning the curriculum. The second component consists of the year-end behavioral objectives for each academic level. The academic divisions which were suggested and accepted by the working committee include the following:

*The use of the letter "k" in the spelling of "Afrika" derives from the Kiswahili language. Its use is a long-standing tradition among many CIBI schools.

	Preschool	**Age Group**
Level One:		2-3½
Level Two:		3-4½
Level Three:		4-5½

	Primary School	**Age Group**
Level One:		5-6½
Level Two:		6-7½
Level Three:		7-8½
Level Four:		8-9½

	Middle School	**Age Group**
Level One:		9-10½
Level Two:		10-11½
Level Three:		11-12½
Level Four:		12-13½

The objectives are year-end objectives and are intended to be adapted by each institution to their respective evaluation/grading periods. The age ranges are generally defined and are not intended to be fixed.

The objectives for each level are arranged within four strands. Those strands are Family, Community, Nation, and Race. The foci for the successive levels are intended to shift from early emphasis on family and self at the preschool levels, to an emphasis on Nation and Race at the middle school levels. This gradual shift is intended to correspond with the natural developmental sequence of children's maturation.

The third component is the instructional guide. The instructional component consists of suggested activities, a list of cognitive skills, an explanation of the Nguzo Saba and recommendations for the organization of lessons, and a Kiswahili glossary.

Component I: Working Definitions

STRAND A - FAMILY

Definition of Family

The family is the basic social unit of society. It is the association of adults and children in a care giving relationship for the purpose of:

- Providing physical protection and development
- Providing mental, emotional and spiritual stability and development
- Politicizing to inspire in the children a desire to build and participate in independent structures that work in the interest of the largest number of Afrikan people at every level of human involvement
- Giving early education and enculturation: developing in the children the intellectual skills and social values that will enable them to build and participate in such structures as described above

Criteria for Evaluating Families

- Provides for physical protection
- Provides for physical development
- Provides for mental stability development
- Provides for emotional stability development
- Provides for spiritual development
- Provides for political development
- Provides for social development

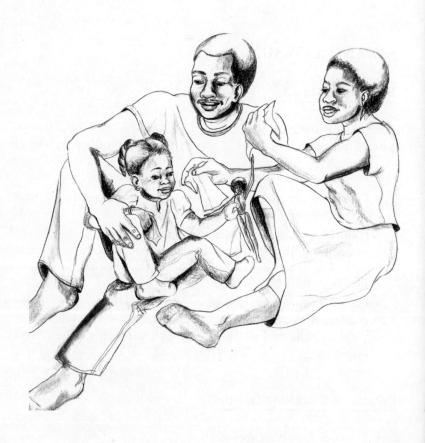

Criteria for Evaluating Leadership in the Family

- Vision — the ability to conceptualize beyond present conditions an idealized future
- Administrative Skills — the ability to organize people and resources for the accomplishment of goals
- Inspirational — the ability to stimulate/motivate people to work in the interest of the family, community, nation and race
- Flexibility — the ability to adapt to changed conditions
- Humility — ability to recognize and accept direction from other members of the community
- Consistency — ability to maintain and practice goals, standards, and values (set by the group) in the face of trials and tribulations over extended periods of time
- Organizational Base — maintains a strong relationship with a viable organization in the community, nation and race
- Traditional Ideas — the active promotion of the traditions and values of the family, community, nation and race
- Correctness of Ideas — ideas are judged by the degree to which those ideas speak to the greatest good for the greatest number of people
- Courageousness — the ability to confront adversity undaunted and unbent

STRAND B - COMMUNITY

Definition of Community

The community is an association of individuals, families and institutions which is defined and delimited by shared history, values, traditions. The functions of the community are to:

- Provide for physical security
- Equitably provide and distribute, for all its members, goods and services which include clothing, food, housing, energy,

health services, sanitation, transportation, education and recreation

- Maintain a system of government which is representative of its people
- Maintain institutions of law and justice that are equally applied to all its members
- Promote a sense of unity wherein its values, and traditions are maintained and reinforced

Criteria for Evaluating Community

- Provides physical security
- Provides goods and services
- Equitably distributes those goods and services
- Maintains a representative governing structure
- Maintains institutions of law and justice
- Promotes a sense of unity

Criteria for Evaluating Leadership in the Community

- Vision – the ability to conceptualize beyond present conditions an idealized future
- Administrative Skills – the ability to organize people and resources for the accomplishment of goals
- Inspirational – the ability to stimulate/motivate people to work in the interest of the family, community, nation and race
- Flexibility – the ability to adapt to changed conditions
- Humility – ability to recognize and accept direction from other members of the community
- Consistency – ability to maintain and practice goals, standards, and values (set by the group) in the face of trials and tribulations over extended periods of time
- Organizational Base – maintains a strong relationship with a viable organization in the community, nation and race

- Traditional Ideas — the active promotion of the traditions and values of the family, community, nation and race
- Correctness of Ideas — ideas are judged by the degree to which those ideas speak to the greatest good for the greatest number of people
- Courageousness — the ability to confront adversity undaunted and unbent

STRAND C - NATION (AFRIKANS IN AMERICA)

Definition of Nation

A nation is an organization of communities which is defined by its shared history, language, and values, existing within a definite geographical area. A nation's functions are:

- To provide physical protection and security for its member communities and institutions
- To develop its natural resources in the best interests of its members
- To equitably distribute the wealth amongst its members
- To foster the maximum development of its human resources in the interest of the national advancement (i.e. effective utilization of available trained and skilled population and the training and educating of the unskilled population)
- To provide a national system for the production of goods and services
- To provide an equitable system for the delivery of goods and services
- To maintain a system of government which is representative of all its people
- To promote national identity and allegiance among all of its members

Criteria for Evaluating the Nation

- Provides physical protection
- Develops natural resources
- Distributes wealth equitably
- Develops human resources
- Provides goods and services
- Distributes goods and services
- Provides representative government
- Promotes national identity

Criteria for Evaluating Leadership in the Nation

- Vision – the ability to conceptualize beyond present conditions to an idealized future
- Administrative Skills – the ability to organize people and resources for the accomplishment of goals
- Inspirational – the ability to stimulate/motivate people to work in the interest of the family, community, nation and race
- Flexibility – the ability to adapt to changed conditions
- Humility – ability to recognize and accept direction from other members of the community
- Consistency – ability to maintain and practice goals, standards, and values (set by the group) in the face of trials and tribulations over extended periods of time
- Organizational Base – maintains a strong relationship with a viable organization in the community, nation and race
- Traditional Ideas – the active promotion of the traditions and values of the family, community, nation and race
- Correctness of Ideas – ideas are judged by the degree to which those ideas speak to the greatest good for the greatest number of people
- Courageousness – the ability to confront adversity undaunted and unbent

STRAND D - RACE

Definition of Race

Race is a division of humanity with similar physical features, similar cultures and common geographical origins. Race is further defined by common history and common political and economic interests.

Guideline to the Study of Race

Origins (Afrikan origin of humanity)
Anthropological discoveries/development
Monogenesis
Mythology
Political and economic determinants

History
Afrikan civilizations in antiquity
Major themes (empire, foreign domination, migration and dispersal, Arabic and European slave trades, colonialism, assimilationism and nationalism)

Goals
National independence
Pan Afrikanism
Rebuilding Afrikan civilization (cultural, economic and political independence)

Criteria for Evaluating Leadership in the Race

- Vision — the ability to conceptualize beyond present conditions an idealized future
- Administrative Skills — the ability to organize people and resources for the accomplishment of goals
- Inspirational — the ability to stimulate/motivate people to work in the interest of the family, community, nation and race

- Flexibility — the ability to adapt to changed conditions
- Humility — ability to recognize and accept direction from other members of the community
- Consistency — ability to maintain and practice goals, standards, and values (set by the group) in the face of trials and tribulations over extended periods of time
- Organizational Base — maintains a strong relationship with a viable organization in the community, nation and race
- Traditional Ideas — the active promotion of the traditions and values of the family, community, nation and race
- Correctness of Ideas — ideas are judged by the degree to which those ideas speak to the greatest good for the greatest number of people
- Courageousness — the ability to confront adversity undaunted and unbent

Component II: Academic Objectives

LEVEL I – PRE-PRIMARY (Ages 2-3½)

Family
1. To identify family members
2. To describe what each member does for one's family
3. To identify family as Afrikan
4. To describe Umoja*
5. To identify members of animal families

Community
1. To describe neighbors
2. To identify students, teachers, parents in school
3. To give name of school and one's own group
4. To describe what members of school do
5. To describe Umoja

Nation
1. To recite school pledges**
2. To name colors of liberation flag
3. To sing 3 liberation songs
4. To identify pictures of Afrikan people in books and magazines
5. To identify freedom fighters from teacher-selected list (born in the United States)
6. To recognize Afrika (shape)
7. To use and respond to Kiswahili greetings / directions
8. To identify Kwanzaa symbols

Race
1. To identify Afrika
2. To identify Afrikan objects and symbols from teacher-selected list
3. To identify continental freedom fighters from teacher-selected list
4. To sing Nguzo Saba song
5. To sing 3 liberation songs
6. To identify black people as Afrikans
7. To identify one country in each region of Afrika

*Umoja, Kujchagulia, Ujima, Ujamaa, Nia, Kuumba, and Imani form the Nguzo Saba (see p. 38)
**The CIBI Pledge is shown in Component III on page 51

LEVEL II — PRE-PRIMARY (Ages 3-4½)

Family
1. To identify self and family members as Afrikan
2. To identify self as a sister or brother
3. To identify family members and describe their functions / roles
4. To describe how the family works in Umoja
5. To identify families in pictures of continental Afrikans (traditional)
6. To draw a picture of the family
7. To recognize animal families

Community
1. To describe neighbors
2. To identify students, teachers, parents in school
3. To give name of school and one's own group
4. To give names of other groups in school
5. To describe functions of school members
6. To give examples of how community needs are met (fire, flood, etc.)
7. To describe Ujima
8. To name two Afrikan ethnic groups
9. To describe (given lesson) the function of community members in traditional Afrikan setting

Nation
1. To recite school pledges
2. To describe liberation flag (Marcus Garvey - contributions, colors)
3. To sing 5 liberation songs
4. To identify pictures of Afrikans in magazines
5. To identify freedom fighters (born in United States) from teacher-selected list and tell about each
6. To recognize shape of Afrika on a world map and a globe
7. To identify "blacks" as Afrikans
8. To use and respond to Kiswahili greetings / directions
9. To identify Kwanzaa symbols
10. To name birth dates of (Malcolm X, M.L. King, etc.) as "holidays"

Race
1. To recognize Afrika on a world map and globe
2. To identify Afrikan continental freedom fighters from teacher-selected lists and tell something about each
3. To identify one country in each region of Afrika
4. To identify Afrikan objects and symbols from teacher-selected lists
5. To draw a picture of Afrikan people
6. To identify "black" people as Afrikan
7. To recite the Nguzo Saba
8. To name freedom fighters no longer living as ancestors

LEVEL III – PRE-PRIMARY (Ages 4-5½)

Family
1. To identify self and family members as Afrikan
2. To identify self as a sister or a brother
3. To describe the role / function of each family member
4. To describe how Umoja works in the family
5. To describe how Ujima works in the family
6. To describe how Ujamaa works in the family
7. To describe Imani
8. To draw a picture of the family
9. To identify families in pictures of continental Afrikans (traditional setting) and describe functions / roles (given appropriate visual aids: picture of Maasai; question what do the mamas do, babas, etc.)
10. To identify pictures of freedom fighters and their families
11. To identify animal families

Community
1. To describe people in the neighborhood
2. To give examples of how community needs are met (fire, flood, etc.)
3. To draw picture of street on which one lives on
4. To draw picture of one's school and the street on which it is located
5. To give names of one's own group and other groups in the school

6. To describe the function / role of each school member
7. To describe Umoja, Ujima, Ujamaa
8. To describe the functions of community members given a picture / story of traditional setting

Nation
1. To recite school pledges
2. To sing seven liberation songs
3. To describe liberation flag
4. To name Afrika as the home of all Afrikans born in the United States
5. To identify freedom fighters (born in United States) from teacher-selected list and tell about each
6. To recognize shape of Afrika on a world map and a globe
7. To identify "blacks" as Afrikan
8. To use and respond to Kiswahili greeting / directions
9. To identify Kwanzaa symbols
10. To name birth dates of (Malcolm X, M.L. King, etc.) as "holidays"

Race
1. To recognize Afrika on a world map and globe
2. To identify continental freedom fighters from teacher-selected lists and tell something about each
3. To identify three countries in each region of Afrika (North, East, South, West)
4. To identify Afrikan objects and symbols from teacher-selected list
5. To draw a picture of Afrikan people
6. To identify "black" people as Afrikan
7. To recite the Nguzo Saba
8. To describe how Afrikans were brought to America
9. To describe freedom fighters and relatives no longer living as ancestors

PRIMARY - LEVEL I (Ages 5-6½)

1. To name and draw pictures of everybody who lives in one's house
2. To state one's first and last names, their meanings and why they were given
3. To state one's age, sex, birth date, address and phone number
4. To state one's age this year, last year and next year
5. To state and illustrate what the members of one's family do in the home
6. To state the age of immediate family members
7. To describe what each person in one's house does all day
8. From one's own family experience, child can answer the following questions:

    Where and from whom do you get your food?

    Why aren't you naked outdoors in the middle of the winter?

    Who provides what you need to keep warm?

    Who put you in this school and why?

    What happens if you get hurt outside playing or if someone fights you and you get hurt?

    What do you do with your family that makes you happy?

    What do you do to make other people in your family happy?

    What have you learned about Afrikan people from your family?

    (For example, celebrations, "innerattainment", symbols in the home, discussions, etc.)

    Who would you like to be like? Why? How can being like that person help Afrikan people?

9. From the responses to the above questions, child can infer the seven criteria for the family
10. To make a flow chart of one's daily routine at home
11. To dramatize a critical and exciting historical segment of an Afrikan person's life
12. To distinguish between correct and incorrect behavior within the family

    Some examples of areas of social behavior which can be focused on are:

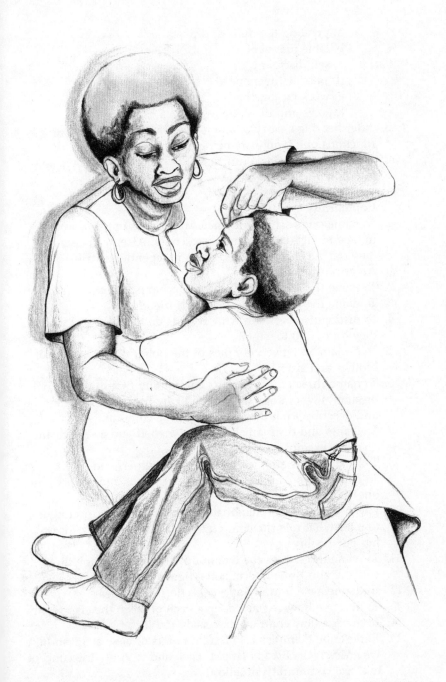

a. greeting to adults and peers
b. table manners
c. self discipline
d. personal hygiene
e. working together
f. goals and direction
13. After hearing a story of a family, to infer and state what functions of a family are being fulfilled, and to judge the extent to which those functions are being fulfilled by using the individual family scale

Community

1. To name one's school and state why one is enrolled in an independent Afrikan American school. Also, to state how long one has been enrolled in an independent Afrikan American school
2. To name five friends and describe what makes them friends
3. To name five things one does with friends
4. To distinguish between what friends do together and what they do not do together
5. To explain and give examples of the political relationship of brother and sister
6. To name three adults in one's community (not in the school or family) whom one likes, to tell why he / she likes them and describe what they each do in the community.
7. To define and distinguish between a good and a service and give five examples of each.
8. To locate goods and services in the neighborhood.
9. To name three Afrikans who produce goods and services in one's community
10. Given the story of a national or Pan Afrikan historical figure, to infer what role the community played in shaping his or her personality
11. To name three ways the community helped to shape three national and three international figures
12. To define a community as a collection of families
13. To describe how we take care of each other in the classroom
14. To make a flow chart of one's daily routine at school
15. To describe examples of different points of view as given in *Why Mosquitoes Buzz in Peoples' Ears,* and to apply the concept to a real community situation

16. To identify north, south, east and west in the community
17. To identify what is north of a given point, south of a given point, etc.

Nation

1. To recite the school and CIBI pledges, and explain in simple terms their meanings
2. To identify the shape of the United States on a map and a globe
3. To identify the United States as the nation in which one lives
4. To describe the ways in which the family helped to shape three national figures, such as Malcolm X
5. To label north, south, east and west on a U.S. map
6. To describe rituals in the school
7. To explain what a pledge is
8. To define what a flag is a symbol of
9. To identify the red, black and green flag as a symbol of unity for Afrikan people. Also, to explain the meaning of its colors.
10. To name Marcus Garvey as the designer and creator of the liberation flag

Race

1. To identify oneself as an Afrikan person
2. To identify Afrika as the traditional homeland of all Afrikan people
3. To identify the shape of Afrika on a map and a globe
4. To use a timeline to identify today, yesterday and tomorrow
5. To distinguish an Afrikan person both from a European and from an Asian
6. To identify on a map and a globe that the earth is covered by land and water
7. To identify and name the four major oceans of the world
8. To identify the continents of the world by shape (identify Europe and Asia as Eurasia)
9. To identify which group of people traditionally come from which continent
10. Given samples of food, clothing, music and or dance of Afrikan, Asian and European cultures, to identify from which culture each is taken

11. To classify pictures (including one of self) of Afrikan and non-Afrikan people
12. To identify self as a member of the Afrikan race
13. Given the story of a Pan Afrikan historical personality, to infer what functions the family played in shaping that personality
14. To name the ways the family helped to shape three Pan Afrikan historical figures
15. To describe how a traditional Afrikan community protected its members
16. To locate north, south, east and west on a world map

PRIMARY - LEVEL II (Ages 6-7½)

Family
1. To recite the seven criteria for family
2. To identify the relationships of mother, father, parent, sister, brother, aunt, uncle, grandparents, and cousins (initially first cousins)
3. To draw those relationships on a family genealogy tree
4. To name one's own family members within all those relationships
5. To describe and represent in pictures or drawings other Afrikan family relationships: matrilineal; patrilineal
6. To identify the geographical boundaries of the traditional nation under study and to identify in what region (north, south, east or west) of the continent it is found
7. To describe and evaluate how that family structure fulfills the seven criteria for family
8. To describe the role the family played in shaping the leadership qualities of Ann Nzingha and Malcolm X (as two examples only)
9. To compare how two Afrikan families within the United States fulfill the seven criteria for family

10. To list the responsibilities one carries out in the home
11. To name and describe the vocation one wishes to pursue and how that vocation can help Afrikan people
12. To make a flow chart of one's daily activities at home (for example, how to tie a shoe, how to button a shirt, how to brush ones teeth, etc.)

Community
1. To define and describe a community giving examples of the criteria for community
2. To identify the city and state in which one lives on a U.S. map
3. Given the story of a traditional Kikuyu community, to infer the seven criteria for a community
4. To apply the seven criteria for a community to the evaluation of their own
5. To define goods and services and give examples of each
6. To locate basic goods and services in ones community or neighborhood
7. To compare the spectrum and quality of goods in one's community with those in other ethnic communities.
8. To identify goods and services that are life giving and life saving and tell which community provides goods and services that are life giving and life saving.
9. To distinguish the cultural nature of the kinds of goods and services in one's community from the cultural nature of the goods and services in other ethnic communities in one's city or town
10. To identify who (what group of people or what key individuals) own or control the production of goods and the distribution of services in one's community
11. To collect and evaluate newspaper clippings of important community events that relate to the Afrikan community where one lives
12. To identify and experience community events that reinforce a sense of unity and Afrikan identity in the community
13. To create and dramatize a series of community events that reinforce a sense of unity
14. To identify examples of issues over which the Afrikan community in one's area is currently struggling

15. To name the city, state and nation in which one resides
16. To define a value, and a value system
17. To describe why a common value system is needed by a community of people
18. To name and define the seven principles of the Nguzo Saba
19. Given a problematic situation, to apply the principles of the Nguzo Saba to solving that problem
20. To describe how Afrikan people in one's neighborhood take care of each other
21. To describe how we take care of each other in the classroom
22. To make flow charts of school routines
23. To identify northeast, northwest, southeast, southwest in the neighborhood

Nation
1. To describe why a common value system is needed in a nation
2. To collect and evaluate newspaper clippings of important national events which impact upon Afrikans in America
3. To infer from historical examples what an Afrikan hero or heroine is
4. To apply the criteria for leadership to five national historical figures or movements
5. To identify five ways in which the family helped to shape three national historical figures
6. To identify five ways in which the community helped to shape three national historical figures
7. To describe how the importance of a national issue (national to Afrikans in America) helped to shape a national hero or heroine
8. To describe the events, issues and purposes of a national resistance movement within the United States (e.g., Turner, Prosser, attempts to take over Florida, Kansas, Oklahoma, the resistance against slavery, etc.)
9. To identify northeast, northwest, southeast, southwest on a U.S. map
10. To define a river and a lake
11. To identify and locate on a U.S. map the major river systems and the Great Lakes of the United States

Race
1. To list five ways a family helped to shape a Pan Afrikan historical figure or movement
2. To list five ways a community helped to shape a Pan Afrikan historical figure or movement
3. To describe the events, issues and purposes of the Haitian revolution
4. To collect and evaluate newspaper clippings pertinent to international issues that relate to Afrikans worldwide
5. To recite school and CIBI pledge and explain their meanings
6. To define a pledge
7. To describe school rituals
8. To distinguish a country from a continent
9. To identify by shape the name and location of the countries of West Afrika
10. To define a continent as a large body of land completely surrounded by water
11. To identify the six continents
12. To locate eight cardinal directions on a world map, a map of Afrika and a map of North America
13. To define an ocean, name the oceans of the world and locate each on a world map

PRIMARY - LEVEL III (Ages 7-8½)

Family
1. To define the functions of a family
2. To apply the seven criteria for a family in evaluating one's own and other families (from literature, history or real life)
3. To identify the following relationships: great grandparents, great-great grandparents, first and second cousins, great aunts and uncles
4. To trace one's own family genealogy three generations removed
5. To represent three generations removed on a genealogy tree or table

6. To explain the relationships of great grandparents (maternal and paternal), great aunts and uncles (maternal and paternal), and great cousins (second, third, fourth, etc.)
7. To write or tell a meaningful story about some member of one's family two or three generations removed (preferably an ancestor)
8. To describe some of the conditions which would keep one from knowing one's full family genealogy
9. To define an ancestor as an Afrikan person who is no longer alive
10. To list and describe responsibilities one carries out in the home
11. To list and describe the vocations one might like to pursue and describe in detail what work someone in that vocation does, and what kind of preparation one must make to achieve that vocation
12. To describe how the vocation can be used by Afrikan people in the community, nation and race
13. To define work as getting a job done efficiently, effectively and with enthusiasm (Reference: Sonia Sanchez, *A Sound Investment*)

Community
1. To name several ancient and modern cities in Afrika
2. To identify whether the city in which they live evolved in response to:
   a. access to a natural waterway
   b. a peculiar characteristic of its terrain or topology
   c. particular social, political or historical conditions
3. To describe the administrative or decision making structure of the city as executive, legislative and judicial
4. To state that a mayor and council members are usually elected by the people
5. To analyze whether members of each branch of city government are Afrikan, and if Afrikan, whether they work in the interests of and in response to the directives of the Afrikan community of that city
6. To list the jobs done by the mayor and the city council
7. To identify the positions involved in the judiciary system
8. To visit a courtroom setting and to evaluate its relation to

Afrikans in the community in terms of whether justice is carried out

9. To compare and contrast a traditional administrative system for reaching executive, legislative and judicial decisions (e.g. Council of Elders) with a contemporary city administrative structure
10. To compare and contrast the administrative structure of a contemporary Afrikan city to that of the city in which they reside (e.g.. Lagos, Dar Es Salaam, Salisbury, Nairobi, etc.)
11. To name and locate on the map the capital cities of the states adjacent to and including the state in which they reside. (Locate capital city as in northern, southern, central, western or eastern region of the state.)
12. To identify the capital cities of the countries of West Afrika and locate them on the map
13. To list common problems of the city, drawing from one's experiences (examples — sanitation problems, water problems, garbage disposal, unemployment, crime, "regentrification")
14. To devise neighborhood-based solutions to some of those problems; solutions in which one can participate
15. To compare and contrast a rural and an urban environment within the U.S.
16. To compare and contrast an urban environment in contemporary Afrika and one in contemporary U.S.
17. To draw on a map how the streets of the city are organized and name how houses are numbered
18. To identify and point out the direction of the school in relation to the dividing line streets for north, south, east and west
19. To distinguish between residential and commercial zones and to identify one of each type of zone by name and location
20. To describe the public transportation system, including types, which ones are used for getting to what areas, and state which would you take, and where would you catch it to get to a specified location?

Nation
1. To define and describe the functions of a nation
2. To cite examples, using historical models, of each of the functions of a nation being fulfilled
3. To describe how the family contributed to the development of three historical personalities among Afrikans in America

4. To describe how the community contributed to the development of three historical personalities among Afrikans in America
5. To describe how a historical figure or movement developed in response to a particular national issue of importance to Afrikans in America
6. To compare an Afrikan family in America and an Afrikan family in some other part of the world
7. To give examples of how several national organizations or institutions developed (e.g., NAACP, Urban League, NBUF, UNIA, RNA, ALSC, NBIPP, AAPRP, CIBI)*: (Also to state their purpose, relationship to Afrikans in America, contribution to Afrika, and contributions to the nation of Afrikans in America.
8. To name and locate the states surrounding their state of residency (to the north, south, east and west)
9. To describe Afrikan American national resistance movements; to define chattel slavery and describe the conditions under which our people were forced to live
10. To describe several organized movements among Afrikans in America to resist slavery by securing, defending and occupying land for the purpose of governing it

Race
1. To describe how the family contributed to the development of a Pan Afrikan historical figure or movement
2. To describe how the community contributed to the development of a Pan Afrikan historical figure or movement
3. To describe how a Pan Afrikan historical figure or movement developed in response to particular national issues
4. To identify, locate and trace on a map of Afrika, and on a world map, the major river systems and lakes of Afrika
5. To describe the historical development of an ancient city of Afrika, and to explain its significance

*National Association for the Advancement of Colored People (NAACP)
National Black United Front (NBUF)
Republic of New Afrika (RNA)
African Liberation Support Committee (ALSC)
National Black Independent Political Party (NBIPP)
All-African People's Revolutionary Party (AAPRP)

PRIMARY - LEVEL IV (Ages 8 - 9½)

Family
1. To name the places where one's parents work; give the phone numbers and describe the work they do
2. To describe examples of Afrikan families who have stayed together through adversity because of their commitment to each other
3. To describe how the Nguzo Saba is practiced in family life
4. To evaluate one's own behavior in the school and at home by the extent to which one practices the Nguzo Saba
5. To describe how people look at situations from different points of view

Community
1. To identify sources of public utility services in the city (water, electricity, sewer, natural gas, etc.)
2. To describe the phases of life known as rites of passage in a traditional Afrikan culture (birth, adulthood, parenthood, eldership, death)
3. To define and give examples of a rite
4. To contrast traditional rites of passage or lack of same in various Afrikan communities, continental and diaspora
5. To describe the roles of each phase within a given culture
6. To identify the countries, terrain, language and other vital statistics relevant to the particular Afrikan culture whose rites of passage are being studied
7. To define and give examples of an age set and what those in an age set share with each other (e.g. experiences). Child can discuss whether there are any parallels for age sets within the culture of Afrikans in America
8. To list and analyze Afrikan youth organizations in one's community in terms of how they fulfill similar roles regarding traditional age sets

Nation
1. To distinguish between natural land formations (continent, island, peninsula, and man-made or political formations such

as a city, state, country or nation)
2. To name 25 states and their capitals
3. To identify a governor as the head of the executive government of a state and to describe his / her duties
   a. To recognize the governor as an elected official
   b. To name the governor of the state in which one resides
4. To identify the state legislature as the legislative body that makes laws for the state
5. To name a number of Afrikan American elected officials at city, state and federal levels who were elected during the Reconstruction period
6. To describe or recount the conditions which led to the election of those officials and to their loss of office
7. To describe the federal system of the United States
8. To contrast the federal system of the United States with those of present day Nigeria and the ancient Kingdom of Kuba
9. To identify the U.S. president as the head of the executive branch of the government; the congress and the senate as the legislative branch; and the Supreme Court as the judicial branch of the national government of the United States
10. To describe the functions of each branch of the federal government
11. To name Afrikan American senators and congressmen
12. To cite decisions made by the Supreme Court that affect the Afrikan community
13. To describe the conditions that led to the establishment of the Congressional Black Caucus
14. To identify the National Black Political Assembly
15. To identify the National Black Independent Political Party (NBIPP) and the National Black United Front (NBUF)
16. To define a gulf, sea, inlet, strait, canal, stream, creek, dam, reservoir
17. To identify and locate on a map and a globe at least one of each kind of waterway
18. To identify the major natural resources of the U.S.

Race
1. To define race
2. To identify and describe racial types
3. To identify and locate on a globe the general location of the

origin of the different races
4. To define racism and cite examples in their community
5. To describe and compare the government, people and economies of Afrikan countries
6. To name 35 Afrikan countries and capitals
7. To describe the history and major figures in the development of ancient Ghana, Mali, Kanem Bornu and Songhay
8. To describe the development of European colonialism and early Afrikan resistance movements (Asante, Dahomey, Angola, Zulu).

MIDDLE SCHOOL - LEVEL I (Ages 9-10½)

Family
1. To define family and list its primary functions
2. To list the seven criteria of family
3. To select a traditional Afrikan family (Maasai, Ibo, Kikuyu, etc.) and compare it with a family in the school community using the seven criteria of family
4. To describe the role of the family in ancient Afrikan society in transmitting values

Community
1. To define community and list its primary functions
2. To list the seven criteria of community
3. To describe and compare a community in traditional Afrikan society and the community one lives in in terms of the way it provides physical security and protection to its members
4. To list goods and services provided by the city in which the school is located
5. To describe and compare the manner in which goods and services are provided by a community in traditional Afrikan society and the community in which the school is located
6. To describe the manner in which the laws of the city are made
7. To determine whether or not the laws are equitably applied to

Afrikans in America (note disproportionate prison population)
8. To identify and describe values, methods and programs of three community institutions that promote unity and carry on tradition
9. To define representative government and to determine whether or not the government of one's city is representative of the interests of the Afrikan community
10. To describe how the geography of different regions of the world affects the manner in which the respective communities of those regions fulfill their community function
11. To be able to locate a given city and state and its directional location on a U.S. map
12. To recite and interpret school pledges and the Nguzo Saba

Nation
1. To define nation and its functions
2. To define and describe the system of chattel slavery
3. To describe the manner in which slavery shaped the national consciousness of Afrikans in America
4. To list the goals of the national liberation struggle of Afrikans in America
5. To evaluate the development of the nation of Afrikans in America using the eight functions of nation as criteria
6. To describe the economic system of the U.S.A. (capital, ownership, private property, division of labor, money, wages, profits, etc.)
7. To describe the economic status of Afrikans in America within the larger economic structure
8. To write a 150 word report on five Afrikans in America who have contributed to the liberation struggle
9. To be able to identify ten Afrikans in America who contributed to the liberation struggle
10. To define leadership
11. To complete a comparative analysis of the leadership of three nineteenth century (pre-civil war) leaders of Afrikans in America

Race
1. To define race
2. To describe the general physical features, common cultural

elements and origins of the three major racial types
3. To list the chief mineral resources of twenty-five Afrikan countries and tell how they are used
4. To define and give three examples of colonialism
5. To describe the relationship of Afrikan resources and European colonialism
6. To describe the liberation movements in five Afrikan countries
7. To identify occurrences in current events which demonstrate the effects of colonialism
8. To prepare a chart on twenty-five Afrikan countries that lists the population, land area, water bodies, chief mineral and agricultural resources and capital cities
9. To locate major cities on the world map using longitude and latitude
10. To name all the countries of Afrika
11. To identify half of the countries and capitals in South America, North America, Europe and Asia
12. To describe the Afrikan origin of science and technology

MIDDLE SCHOOL - LEVEL II (Ages 10-11½)

Family
1. To define family and its functions
2. To list seven criteria for family
3. To complete a comparative analysis of several Afrikan families (American, continental, Caribbean), using the seven criteria
4. To describe the way in which the families of Malcolm X and King prepared them for the roles they eventually played in the liberation struggle of Afrikans in America
5. To describe the family organization found in pre-colonial Afrika and China

Community
1. To define community and list its primary functions
2. To list the seven criteria of community
3. To complete a comparative analysis of several Afrikan

communities (in America, the Caribbean, on the continent),
using the seven criteria for community

4. To describe in detail the manner in which services are
provided by the local government (policy making,
administration, implementation)

5. To give examples of policies and administrative decisions
regarding public services by the local government which have
adversely affected the Afrikan community

6. To describe the legislative process of the local government and
how Afrikans may influence that process (voting, lobbying,
demonstrations, petitions, etc.)

7. To give examples of how political actions by the Afrikan
community have influenced the legislative and administrative
process of the local government

8. To describe the judiciary of the local government

9. To identify and describe values, methods and programs of
three community institutions that promote unity and carry on
traditions

10. To write a research paper on the city in which the school is
located (land area, population, founding date, chief products,
type of government, brief history)

11. To write a short history of Afrikans in the city in which the
school is located detailing origin of Afrikan populations,
migration patterns, key individuals and institutions, and
present status of the Afrikan population

Nation

1. To define nation and its functions

2. To describe chattel slavery in America and its consequences for
the Afrikan population

3. To describe four major slave revolts, including the leadership,
motivations and outcomes of each

4. To define and describe *defacto* or neo-slavery

5. To compare chattel slavery to defacto slavery using case
studies (Reference notes: *Roots* before and after the civil war,
slave narratives, sharecroppers, migrants, laborers, unskilled
urban Afrikan laborers.)

6. To evaluate the development of a nation of Afrikans in
America using the eight functions of nation as criteria

7. To describe and compare political economic systems of the west and of traditional Afrika (democracy, dictatorship, monarchy, communalism)
8. To describe the political economic status of Afrikans in America
9. To write a 150 word composition on ten Afrikans in America who contributed to the liberation struggle in America
10. To identify twenty Afrikans in America who contributed to the liberation struggle in America
11. To define leadership and complete a comparative analysis on five post-civil war nineteenth century leaders
12. To describe efforts of Afrikans in America to establish independent schools and other institutions in the pre-civil war era

Race
1. To define race
2. To describe the three principal races of the world
3. To describe how the European "scientific" conception of race is used as a tool of cultural, political and economic imperialism
4. To define and describe monogenesis
5. To describe ancient Ethiopian and other pre-historic Sudanic cultures of Afrika
6. To describe the leadership, the political / economic, scientific and architectural accomplishments of ancient Egyptian civilization during the 1st through the 6th dynasties
7. To describe the paleontological, archaeological and anthropological discoveries that confirm the Afrikan origin of humanity
8. To describe the cultural unity of ancient Ethiopia / Egypt and traditional Afrika
9. To describe the early civilizations of India and China
10. To complete a geographical chart on all fifty-two continental Afrikan countries (population, land area, water bodies, chief resources, capital cities, former colonial power, present leadership, major political party, and days of independence)
11. To complete a geographical chart on ten Afrikan nations in the Caribbean and South America
12. To locate major cities on the globe using longitude and latitude
13. To locate all oceans, seas, gulfs, large island, continents, hemispheres, countries and major cities of the world

MIDDLE SCHOOL - LEVEL III (Ages 11-12½)

Family
1. To describe family and its functions
2. To list the seven criteria of family
3. To describe the impact of slavery on the Afrikan family
4. To list three socio-economic factors which affect the forms and functions of the family of Afrikans in America
5. To describe four forms of the family among Afrikans in America (single parent, nuclear, extended, polygamous)
6. To define and give examples of matriarchy and patriarchy
7. To describe the matriarchial family tradition among the Ashanti and the Swazi

Community
1. To define community and list its primary functions
2. To list the seven criteria of community
3. To describe ways that tribal or national policy of the Ashanti and Zulu nations affected the population at the village level
4. To examine, in Tanzania and Mozambique, interaction between the villages and the national government in the determination to proceed with the development of the Ujamaa collective farms
5. To identify and examine the input and influence of individuals, groups and businesses in the legislative arm of the local city government
6. To identify the most influential elements (individuals, organizations, institutions) of the local community of Afrikans in America
7. To describe how those influential elements individually and collectively determine the political orientation of the Afrikan community
8. To identify the major centers of financial and political power in the affairs of the city where the school is located
9. To identify, through research, how those individuals and institutions may have used their influence to the detriment of the Afrikan community

10. To identify and evaluate means whereby the traditional Afrikan community whose values were intact was able to avoid inequitable policy making because of power politics (emphasize communalist traditions, size of community)

Nation
1. To define nation and its functions
2. To describe the development of the contemporary western conception of nation
3. To contrast the respective levels of political development in western Europe and Afrika during the 15th and 16th Centuries A.D.
4. To analyze the comparative characteristics of Afrikan nations using the listed criteria for nations; and to show how the Afrikan nations were less developed in key areas that permitted the European conquest
5. To describe several efforts of Afrikan nations during the 14th through 19th centuries to strengthen their nations and avoid European conquest and domination
6. To define nationalism
7. To describe the history of nationalist thought and activity within the Afrikan community in the U.S.A.
8. To name the most prominent nationalist thinkers among Afrikans in America over the last two centuries
9. To describe the historical circumstance that occasioned the prevalent name used to describe Afrikans in America over the last three centuries
10. To describe the scope and significance of electoral politics among Afrikans in America
11. To describe the current status of Afrikans in America in the areas of employment, income, education, health and housing
12. To describe the economic and political difficulties encountered by the newly independent nations of Afrika
13. To compare development plans for Afrikans in America formulated by different national Afrikan American leaders

Race
1. To define race and give a short written history of race in international politics

2. To define mulatto and miscegenation and describe their historical consequences for Afrika and its people
3. To define culture and describe its role in international politics
4. To describe the historical periods delineated by Chancellor Williams and the rationale for each
5. To define the diaspora
6. To describe the development of Pan Afrikanism
7. To describe the ideological works of major Pan Afrikan personalities and institutions in the development of Pan Afrikanism
8. To describe the development of the Organization of African Unity (OAU)
9. To name and describe three regional economic and political associations in Afrika and the Caribbean
10. To describe the trade patterns between Afrikan nations and their former European colonial masters
11. To identify and describe major international developments in politics, economics and science, and the impact of those developments on Afrika and its people
12. To describe the items of trade, including strategic resources, that Afrikan countries process
13. To identify and describe the major Afrikan population centers and their respective growth patterns

MIDDLE SCHOOL - LEVEL IV (Ages 12-13½)

Family
1. To describe family and its functions
2. To describe the current status of the Afrikan family and the economic, social, political and spiritual factors affecting it
3. To define and describe the responsibilities of parenting
4. To describe the role of values in building strong Afrikan families
5. To describe the significance of rites of passage in traditional societies and their relevance today
6. To distinguish family and household

Community
1. To describe community and list its primary functions
2. To identify and analyze the major centers of economic and political power in one's home city
3. To examine and analyze the nature of the impact that those power centers have on the Afrikan community
4. To examine the response of the Afrikan community and its leadership to those power centers in nationalist and an assimilationist perspectives
5. To devise theoretical solutions (including necessary resources for implementation) to the problems confronting the African community and compare those plans with those of the current community leadership
6. To describe the sources of values / morals within our community
7. To describe the impact of illicit drugs and alcohol on our community and the socio-political climate which permits them to flourish
8. To define independent institutions and describe the role they play in developing a self determined Afrikan community

Nation
1. To define nation and its functions
2. To describe the current political and economic status of Afrikans in America and provide a historical background for the current status
3. To describe the historical development of nationalism among Afrikans in America
4. To describe the evolution of the federal government of the U.S.A. and its impact on the Afrikan population
5. To describe the history of the civil rights struggle by Afrikans and their supporters in the U.S.A
6. To describe the impact of Afrikans in electoral politics at the national level
7. To examine the viability of electoral politics as a primary solution to the problems confronting Afrikans in America
8. To define institutional racism and describe the psychological, spiritual, economic and political impact on the lives of Afrikans in America

9. To describe the Haitian revolution and its significance for Afrikans in America
10. To describe the form and content of traditional Afrikan spiritual systems, and their current status
11. To describe the origin and historical relationship of the so-called world religions (Christianity, Islam, Judaism) with Afrikan societies
12. To examine the role of religion in the resistance movement and civil rights structures of Afrikans in America

Race
1. To describe the historical development of Pan Afrikanism in Afrika and the diaspora
2. To describe the two aspects of Pan Afrikanism (continental, transoceanic) and their ideological significance for Afrikans in America
3. To write out and describe the rationale for the historical periods of Afrikan history as prepared by Chancellor Williams
4. To write out a timeline detailing the major events and trends of each historical period of Afrikan and world history
5. To describe the role of race and culture in Afrika's political economy
6. To describe the role of race and culture in the political economy of the U.S.A.
7. To describe the role of race and culture in the world order
8. To describe the relationship of international agencies (United Nations, World Bank, International Monetary Fund, etc.) to Afrikan development
9. To define neo-colonialism and describe the history of its development
10. To analyze the major ideological and economic theories of the world and compare their impact in different Afrikan countries
11. To define and analyze white supremacy, identifying its origins, forms, effects, and responses.

Component III: Instructional Guide

Effective instructional strategy requires that the mwalimu (teacher), mzazi (parent), or interested person be aware of the several cognitive dimensions of teaching and learning. The Taxonomy of the Cognitive Dimension of Social Studies is included here in order to facilitate the comprehensive learning experience. The skills and objectives which were listed earlier in this document should be taught with the hierarchy of learning - thinking levels in mind. The mwalimu should prepare each teaching - learning experience with precise levels of cognition structured into the lesson plan.

Taxonomy of the Cognitive Dimension of Social Studies

RECOGNITION

Details
> Mwanafunzi (student) is required to identify and name facts such as countries, cities, personalities and dates.

Definitions
> Mwanafunzi is asked to define important terms.

Comparison
> Mwanafunzi is requested to identify likenesses and differences.

Sequence
> Mwanafunzi is required to identify proper historical sequence and identify differences between periods.

Cause and Effect
> Mwanafunzi is required to recall explicitly stated causes and their consequences regarding historical and social occurrences.

TRANSLATION

Details
> Mwanafunzi can draw or otherwise represent important facts, including political maps, government organization flow charts, etc.

Definitions
> Mwanafunzi rephrases or restates the definition of major concepts in his / her own words.

Comparison
> Mwanafunzi represents in graphic or other form the comparison of certain facts or concepts.

Sequence
> Mwanafunzi can draw a timeline of historical occurrences.

Cause and Effect
> Mwanafunzi is required to restate in his / her own words the cause and consequence of given social / historical occurrences.

INTERPRETATION

Details
> Mwanafunzi will be required to compose and differentiate descriptive details of geography, nationality, personalities in an essay and with the use of graphs, charts, etc.

Definitions
> Mwanafunzi will be requested to relate given concepts to current and historical events.

Cause and Effect
> Mwanafunzi is required to differentiate and categorize the events and dynamics that led to different results.

APPLICATION

Detail
> Mwanafunzi will be requested to construct hypothetical communities, nations, etc., and, given hypothetical socio-economic scenarios, illustrate the general interactions and outcomes.

Definition
> Mwanafunzi is able to formulate generalities or historical laws given the specific historical information.

EVALUATION

Fact or Opinion
> Mwanafunzi will be expected to analyze and assess the factuality of a given statement based on general knowledge.

Adequacy and Validity
> Given a general knowledge of subject and appropriate criteria, the mwanafunzi will be expected to evaluate the adequacy and validity of actual or hypothetical actions.

Worth, Desirability and Acceptability
> Mwanafunzi will be expected to judge the worth, desirability and acceptability of real and hypothetical actions and behaviors.

> Mwanafunzi will be expected to evaluate a set of circumstances, determine the probability of specific occurrences and justify the prediction. The mwanafunzi will also be expected to make explicit recommendations based on facts, analysis and reasoning.

Nguzo Saba

All human experience occurs in the context of culture. Learning and instruction are very much culture bound and determined. In fact, formal learning and teaching are critical components in the perpetuation of culture. In the Afrocentric or Pan Afrikanist oriented schools, the Nguzo Saba serves as the focus of personal and collective values, traditions, and actions within the Afrikan and Afrikan American cultural experience. The Nguzo Saba has gained a broad acceptance since its introduction by Maulana Karenga. It is uniquely suited to serve as a vehicle for the expression and consequently the teaching of those values central to our overall mission of attaining real self sufficiency for Afrikan people, and building a more beautiful world in the process. Listed below are the principles of the Nguzo Saba with sample statements of objectives which should be included along with the content objectives, and cognitive objectives in the preparation of the comprehensive learning experience.

UMOJA (UNITY)

Family
>To maintain the integrity of the family
>To display attitudes of mutual respect, selflessness, collectivism and cooperativeness
>To maintain open and honest intra-family communication
>To support and encourage the development of each family member's potential
>To speak and act as a unit

Community and Race
>To strive for consensus after thorough analysis, constructive criticism
>To support viable efforts to promote and maintain unified national and racial action

KUJICHAGULIA (SELF DETERMINATION)

Family & Individual
>To maintain an Afrikan centered cultural orientation through family ritual and other formal and informal activities
>To remain alert, active and creative in family's financial, legal and social responsibilities
>To construct or coordinate home projects that promote self sufficiency, e.g., gardening, home repairs, furniture rehabilitation and construction, sewing, etc.

Community and Race
>To create, maintain and support Afrikan centered institutions of culture, politics, finance, industry, etc. To increase the degree of independence within the community, nation and race.

UJIMA (COLLECTIVE WORK & RESPONSIBILITY)

Family
> To make our brothers' and sisters' problems our own and to solve them together
> To share work and responsibilities for family projects, goals or mission

Community, Nation and Race
> To share in the work and responsibilities of the collective effort to advance the community, nation and race

UJAMAA (COOPERATIVE ECONOMICS)

Family & Individual
> To plan joint economic activities
> To pool resources for the advancement of the family and its several members

Community, Nation & Race
> To pool our resources in such a way as to maximize the development of business ventures and the creation of jobs
> To maintain the economic viability of our enterprises with enthusiastic and critical support

NIA (PURPOSE)

Family & Individual
> To adopt a life priority of building and developing the community and nation
> To promote, as a family priority, the development of independent Afrikan centered institutions

Community, Nation & Race
> To adopt as a collective mission, the full development of an independent self sufficient nation

KUUMBA (CREATIVITY)

Family & Individual
To maintain ourselves and our homes in an orderly, hygenic and aesthetically pleasing way at all times

Community, Nation & Race
To make our institutions and communities as beautiful and orderly as possible and to maintain that condition

IMANI (FAITH)

Family & Individual
To believe strongly in our ability to accomplish all that we want
To believe that our collective effort is just and correct and that it warrants our unqualified support

Community, Nation & Race
To believe in and support the collective wisdom or our ancestors, elders and leaders
To foster in our communities a general faith in and commitment to the ultimate victory of our struggle

Preparing the Lesson

The inclusive and dynamic nature of social studies requires a "multi-tasking" approach to actual instruction. The subject content, cognition and problem solving, and cultural values are coequal components and must therefore receive roughly coequal emphasis in delivery. The concept of multi-tasking implies several discrete objectives that are distinct but interrelated and which are accomplished in the same lesson activity. In real life these components are not discrete, but their separation in theory serves to maximize the effectiveness of instruction.

Sample Lesson Plan

A) Subject Content
    Middle School Level III, Family
    Objective: To describe the impact of slavery on the Afrikan family in America

B) Cognition & Problem Solving
    Interpretation: Cause and Effect
    Objective: To differentiate and categorize events and dynamics that led to specific results

C) Cultural Values and Principles
    Nguzo Saba, Umoja
    Objective: To understand and appreciate the need to maintain the integrity of the family

Lesson Materials

Video tapes: "Half Slave Half Free," starring Avery Brooks; "Roots Vol I-IV"; "Freedom Road," starring Muhammad Ali

Reading: Slave narratives, autobiography of Frederick Douglass

Lesson Activity: Teacher-directed discussion of video and / or reading, oral evaluation, given criteria for evaluating family, by class

Follow-up Activity: Essay on destructive impact of slavery and resilience of Afrikan family with relevant lessons for the contemporary Afrikan family

The several components that make up the lesson plan include the a.) content objective, b.) materials, c.) activity, d.) valuing objective and e.) skills objective. These components are fused at the direction of the mwalimu with the interaction of the mwanafunzi. As indicated in the diagram, the mwalimu must remain cognizant of extracurricular input which include parent / family, school, and community. These additional inputs are important determinants of the long-term, permanent effect on the mwanafunzi's behavior. The evaluation of the lesson itself will be gauged according to the performance criteria of the initial components of the lesson.

SAMPLE LESSON PLAN

LESSON TITLE:
IMPACT OF SLAVERY ON THE
AFRIKAN AMERICAN FAMILY

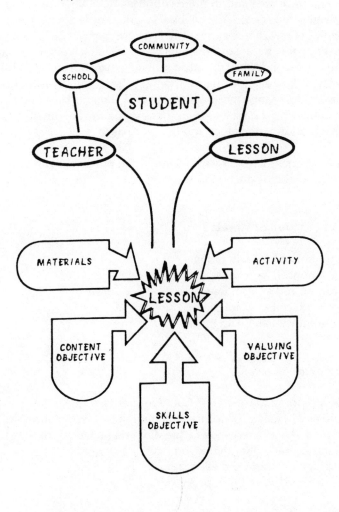

Kiswahili

Kiswahili is an east Afrikan language. It is spoken over a broader geographical area and in more countries than any other traditional Afrikan language. It is the national language of Tanzania. It is spoken widely in Kenya and Uganda, and is used in parts of Zaire, Congo and Mozambique. Because of the international character of the language, many independent Afrocentric schools have chosen Kiswahili as a principal language in their curricula. These schools recognize the primary role language plays in cultural transmission and provide Kiswahili as a means of strengthening the mwanafunzi's personal identification with values and things Afrikan.

Some frequently used Kiswahili terms and phrases are provided here as a general introduction to the language.

Pronunciation of Vowels

a pronounced as 'a' in father
e pronounced as 'a' in day
i pronounced as 'e' in Egypt
o pronounced as 'o' in go
u pronounced as 'oo' in moon

Greetings

Habari gani - How are you? (more formal greeting)
Hujambo - Hello (less formal; literally - have you any troubles?)
Sijambo - Hello (in response, literally - no I have no troubles)
Njema asante - Fine, thank you
Tutaonana - Until we meet again
Baki na heri - Remain in peace

Manners

Tafadhali - Please
Sikitu - It's nothing
Ndio - Yes
Asante sana - Thank you very much
Nisamehe - Excuse me
La, hapana - No

Waut (People)

Ndugu - Brother
Baba - Father
Mwalimu - Teacher
Dada - Sister
Mama - Mother
Mwanafunzi - Student

Concepts

Nguzo Saba - Seven Principles
Adui - Enemy
Shabaha - Aim, goal
Utaratibu - System, organization
Kujitawala - Self rule
Elimu - Education
Njuzi - Knowledge
Mumba Dunia - Creator of the Earth
Viongozi - Leaders
Amani - Peace
Kazi - Work

CIBI PLEDGE

We are Afrikan people struggling for national liberation,

We are preparing leaders and workers to bring about positive change for our people,

We stress the development of our bodies, minds, souls and consciousness,

Our commitment is to self-determination, self-defense and self-respect for our race.

References

Aardemay, Verna (1975) *Why Mosquitoes Buzz in Peoples' Ears.* New York: Dial Books for Young Readers.

Achebe, Chinua (1958) *Things Fall Apart.* London: Heinemann.

Asante, Molefi. (1987) *The Afrocentric Idea.* Philadelphia: Temple University Press.

Asante, Molefi. (1988) *Afrocentricity.* Trenton: Africa World Press.

Diop, Cheikh Anta (1974) *The African Origin of Civilization.* New York: Lawrence Hill and Company.

Diop, Cheikh Anta (1987) *The Cultural Unity of Black Africa.* Chicago: Third World Press.

Douglass, Frederick (1845) *Narrative of the Life of Frederick Douglass, an American Slave.* Boston.

Esedebe, P. Olisanwuche (1982) *Pan Africanism: The Idea and Movement, 1776-1963.* Washington: Howard University Press.

Garvey, Amy Jacques (1969) *The Philosophy and Opinions of Marcus Garvey.* New York: Atheneum.

Gifford, Prosser and Louis, William Roger, eds. (1982) *The Transfer of Power in Africa: Decolonization 1940-1960.* New Haven: Yale University Press.

Haley, Alex (1965) *Autobiography of Malcolm X.* New York: Ballantine Books.

Haley, Alex (1976) *Roots.* Garden City, N.Y.: Doubleday & Co., Inc.

Karenga, Maulana (1982) *Introduction to Black Studies.* Los Angeles: Kawaida Publications.

Kunjufu, Jawanza (1987) *Lessons From History: A Celebration in Blackness* (Elementary and High School Editions) Chicago: African American Images.

Jackson, John G. (1970) *Introduction to African Civilization.* New York: Citadel Press.

Madhubuti, Haki R. (1978) *Enemies: The Clash of Races.* Chicago: Third World Press.

Mellon, James, ed. (1988) *Bullwhip Days.* New York: Weidenfield & Nicholson.

Obadele, Imari A. (1987) *A Beginner's Outline of the History of Afrikan People.* Washington: The House of Songhay.

Rogers, J.A. (1972) *World's Great Men of Color, Vols I and II.* New York: Collier Books / MacMillian Publishing Co.

Sanchez, Sonia (1980) *A Sound Investment.* Chicago: Third World Press.

Sertima, Ivan Van, ed. (1988) *Great Black Leaders: Ancient and Modern.* U.S.A: Journal of Afrikan Civilizations Ltd., Inc.

Stuckey, Sterling (1972) *The Ideological Origins of Black Nationalism,* Boston: Beacon Press.

Subira, George (1986) *Black Folks Guide to Business Success.* Newark: Very Serious Business Enterprise.

Sundiata, Kieta Tarharka (1972) *Black Manhood: The Building of Civilization by the Black Man of the Nile.* Washington: University Press of America

Williams, Chancellor (1974) *Destruction of Black Civilization.* Chicago: Third World Press.

ISBN: 0-932415-48-2 PB $7.9

*I find the curriculum guide conceptually Afrocentric and exciting. Indeed the work in this guide is the resu
of years of practice and research. What we have come to learn over the last few years is that African America
children do learn effectively from culturally consistent models of education. That is the way all children lear
This guide should influence the discussion of the proper education of our children well into the next millenium*

Molefi Kete Asante
author, *AFROCENTRICITY* and the *AFROCENTRIC IDEA*

*CIBI has taken a major step in the liberation of our people with their Social Studies Curriculum. It's well balance
between afrocentricity and critical thinking skills. In most cities, we have African mayors, superintendents
principals, teachers, and students but a white Euro-centric curriculum remains in place. CIBI needs to b
commended and supported.*

Jawanza Kunjufu
author, *COUNTERING THE CONSPIRACY TO DESTROY BLACK BOYS*